MEDITATIONS TO HEAL YOUR LIFE

MEDITATIONS TO
HEAL YOUR LIFE

Louise L. Hay

HAY HOUSE, INC.
CARLSBAD, CA

Published and distributed in the United States by:

Hay House, Inc., P.O. Box 5100, Carlsbad, CA 92018-5100
(800) 654-5126 • (800) 650-5115 (fax)

Library of Congress Cataloging-in-Publication Data

Hay, Louise L.
       Meditations to heal your life / Louise L. Hay.
              p.   cm.
       ISBN   1-56170-106-8 :
       1. Meditations.   2. Affirmations.   3. Mental healing.   I. Title.
   BL624.2.H38   1994
291.4 ' 3--dc20   94-26019
                                                                 CIP

ISBN 1-56170-106-8

00 01 99 98   5 4 3 2
First Printing, December 1994
Second Printing, February 1998

Printed in the United States of America

CONTENTS

Introduction

This is a book of ideas to spark our own creative thinking process. It gives us an opportunity to see other ways to approach our experiences. We come into this world with such a pure, clear mind, totally connected with our inner wisdom. As we grow, we pick up fears and limitations from the adults around us. By the time we reach adulthood, we have a lot of negative beliefs that we are not even aware of. And, we tend to build our lives and our experiences upon these false beliefs.

As you read this book, you may find statements that you do not agree with. They may clash with your own belief systems. That is all right. It is what I call "stirring up the pot." You do not have to agree with everything I say. But please examine what you believe and why. This is how we grow and change.

When I first began on my pathway, I used to challenge many of the metaphysical things that I heard. The more I examined my own beliefs in relation to the new ideas, the more I realized that I believed many things that were contributing to the unhappiness in my life. As I began to release the old, negative concepts, my life also changed for the better.

Begin anywhere in this book. Open it at will. The message will be perfect for you at that moment. It may confirm what you already believe, or it may challenge you. It is all part of the growth process. You are safe and all is well.

I dwell in a world

of love and

acceptance.

I radiate acceptance.

If I want to be accepted as I am, then I need to be willing to accept others as they are. We always want to have our parents accept us totally, and yet often we are not willing to accept them as they are. Acceptance is giving ourselves and others the ability to just be. It is arrogant to set standards for others. We can only set standards for ourselves. And even then, we want them to be more like guidelines than standards. The more we can practice self-acceptance, the easier it is to drop habits that no longer serve us. It is easy for us to grow and change in an atmosphere of love.

I claim my power

and move

beyond all

limitations.

I forgive myself, and I set myself free.

Heavy dependence upon anything outside myself is addiction. I can be addicted to drugs and alcohol, to sex and tobacco; and I can also be addicted to blaming people or judging people, to illness, to debt, to being a victim, to being rejected. Yet, I can move beyond these things. Being addicted is giving up my power to a substance or a habit. I can always take my power back. This is the moment I take my power back! I choose to develop the positive habit of knowing that life is here for me. I am willing to forgive myself and move on. I have an eternal spirit that has always been with me, and it is here with me now. I relax and let go, and I remember to breathe as I release old habits and practice positive new ones.

Life loves me and

I am safe.

I communicate freely.

It is safe for me to grow up. I love to learn and grow and change, and I feel safe in the midst of it all, knowing that change is a natural part of life. My personality is flexible, and it is easy for me to go with the flow of life. My inner being is consistent; therefore, I am safe in every kind of experience. When I was a little child, I did not know what the future would bring. As I now begin my journey into adulthood, I realize that tomorrow is equally unknown and mysterious. I choose to believe that it is safe for me to grow up and take charge of my life. My first adult act is to learn to love myself unconditionally, for then I can handle whatever the future may bring.

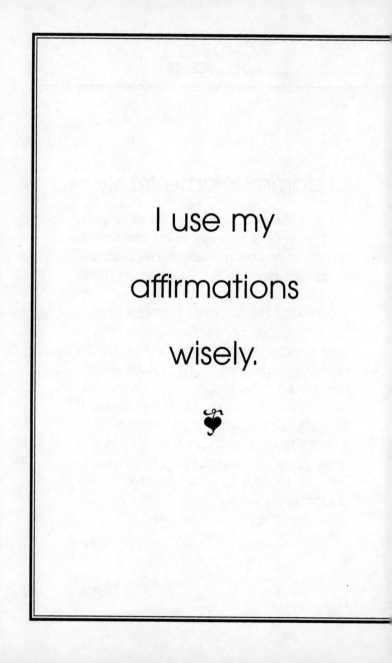

I use my

affirmations

wisely.

In the Beginning is the Word.

Every single thought I have and every sentence I speak is an affirmation. It's either positive or negative. Positive affirmations create positive experiences, and negative affirmations create negative experiences. A tomato seed, if planted, will only grow into a tomato plant. An acorn will only grow into an oak tree. A puppy will only grow into a dog. If we continually repeat negative statements about ourselves or about life, we only keep producing more negative experiences. I now rise beyond my family habit of seeing life in a negative way. My new affirmation habit is to only speak of the good I want in my life. Then only good will come to me.

No matter what
my challenge, I
know I am loved.

This too shall pass, and we will grow and benefit from it!

We are literally walking through uncharted waters here. And everyone involved is doing the best they can with the knowledge and understanding that they have at this point in time and space. Be proud of yourself for doing more than you thought you could. Remember that someone, somewhere, on this planet, has been healed of every single dis-ease that we've been able to create. There has to be a healing answer. It doesn't matter what language you speak. Love speaks to us all from the heart. Spend time every day just quieting down and feeling the love from your heart going through your arms and legs and through every organ in your body. Love is a healing power. Love opens all doors. Love is an ever-ready Universal Power that is here to help us overcome every challenge in our lives. Open your heart. Let the love flow. Feel your Oneness with the Power that created you.

I am the main

authority

in my world.

I am the author of my life.

No person, place, or thing has any power over me, for I am the only thinker in my mind. As a child I accepted authority figures as gods. Now I am learning to take back my power and become my own authority figure. I now accept myself as a powerful, responsible being. As I meditate every morning, I get in touch with my own inner wisdom. The school of life is deeply fulfilling as we come to know that we are all students and all teachers. We each have come to learn something and to teach something. As I listen to my thoughts, I gently guide my mind toward trusting my own Inner Wisdom. Grow and blossom and entrust all your affairs on Earth to your Divine Source. All is well.

I go beyond

barriers into

possibilities.

There are no barriers to my life.

The gateways to wisdom and learning are always open, and more and more I am choosing to walk through them. Barriers, blocks, obstacles, and problems are personal teachers giving me the opportunity to move out of the past and into the Totality of Possibilities. I love stretching my mind, thinking of the highest good imaginable. As my mind can conceive of more good, the barriers and blocks dissolve. My life becomes full of little miracles popping up out of the blue. And every now and then, I give myself permission to do absolutely nothing but sit and be open to Divine Wisdom. I am a student of life, and I love it.

Flowers, like people,

are all beautiful in

their own way

and constantly

unfolding.

Beauty arouses me and heals me.

Beauty is everywhere. Natural beauty shines forth from every little flower, from the patterns of reflected light on the surface of water, from the quiet strength of old trees. Nature thrills me, renews and refreshes me. I find relaxation, enjoyment, and healing in the simplest things in life. As I look with love at nature, I find it easy to look with love at myself. I am part of nature; thus, I am beautiful in my own unique way. Wherever I look, I see beauty. Today I resonate with all the beauty in life.

My bills are an
affirmation of my
ability to pay.

I pay my way easily.

The power that created us has put everything here for us. It is up to us to deserve and to accept. Whatever we have now is what we have accepted. If we want something different or more or less, we don't get it by complaining; we can only get something different by expanding our consciousness. Welcome all your bills with love, and rejoice as you write out the checks, knowing that what you're sending out is coming back to you multiplied. Start feeling positive about this issue. Bills are really wonderful things. It means that somebody has trusted you enough to give you their service or product, knowing that you have the ability to pay for it.

My body is a good

friend that I take

loving care of.

I love my body.

My body is perfect for me at this time. My body weight is also perfect. I am exactly where I choose to be. I am beautiful, and every day I become more attractive. This concept used to be very hard for me to accept, yet things are changing now that I am treating myself as if I were someone who was deeply loved. I'm learning to reward myself with healthy little treats and pleasures now and again. Little acts of love nurture me, doing things that I really like, such as quiet time, a walk in nature, a hot soothing bath, or anything that really gives me pleasure. I enjoy caring for myself. I believe it is okay to like myself and to be my own best friend. I know my body is filled with star light and that I sparkle and glow everywhere I go.

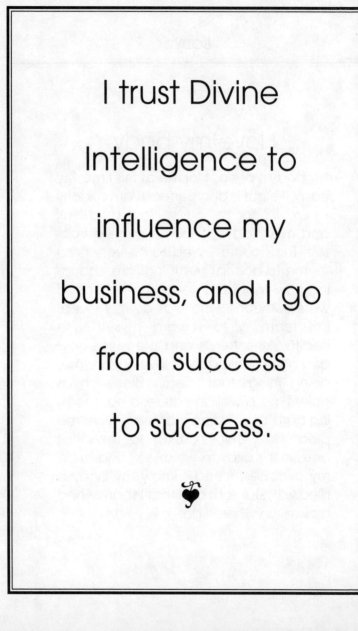

I trust Divine Intelligence to influence my business, and I go from success to success.

My business is doing what I love.

I trust Divine Intelligence to run my business. Whether I own my own business in a worldly sense or not, I am an instrument employed by this Divine Intelligence. There is only One Intelligence, and this Intelligence has a splendid track record in the history of our solar system, guiding each of the planets for millions of years along pathways that are orderly and harmonious. I willingly accept this Intelligence as my partner in business. It is easy for me to channel my energy into working with this Powerful Intelligence. Out of this Intelligence comes all the answers, all the solutions, all the healings, all the new creations and ideas that make my business such a joyous blessing and success.

I am a competent

driver and a

friendly

passenger.

I love my car.

Driving is a safe and pleasant experience for me. I take good care of my car,
and my car takes good care of me. It is
ready to go whenever I am. I have the
perfect mechanic, who also loves my
car. I fill my car with love whenever I
enter it, so love is always traveling with
me. I send love to other drivers on the
road, as we are all traveling together.
Love goes before me, and love greets
me at my destination.

Take care of

yourself the best

you can.

I am a shining light.

My body is a miracle. The bodies of the people I care for are also miracles. Our bodies know how to handle emergencies, and they know how to rest and replenish themselves. We are learning to listen to our bodies and to give our bodies what they need. Sometimes caring for others is an overwhelming job. It is more than we had anticipated. Learn to ask for help. Whether you are a caregiver or a care-receiver, loving yourself is one of the most important things you can do. When you truly love and accept yourself exactly as you are, it's as though you shift gears on some level. Suddenly, you can relax and know, deep in your heart, that All Is Well.

I change my

thinking

with love.

I change my life when I change my thinking.

We are Light. We are Spirit. We are wonderful, capable beings, all of us. And it is time for us to acknowledge that we create our own reality. We create our reality with our minds. If we want to change our reality, then it's time for us to change our minds. We do this by choosing to think and speak in new and positive ways. I learned a long time ago that if I would change my thinking, I could change my life. Changing our thinking is really dropping our limitations. As we drop our limitations, we begin to be aware of the Infinity of life all around us. We begin to understand that we are already perfect, whole, and complete. Each day gets easier.

No matter what happened in the past, I begin now to allow the tiny child inside to blossom and to know that it is deeply loved.

It is safe for me to grow up.

We are all beloved children of the Universe, and yet there are dreadful things happening, such as child abuse. It is said that 30 percent of our population has experienced child abuse. This is not something new. We are at a point right now where we are beginning to allow ourselves to be aware of things that we used to conceal behind walls of silence. These walls are starting to come down so that we can make changes. Awareness is the first step in making changes. For those of us who had really difficult childhoods, our walls and our armors are very thick and strong. Still, behind our walls, the little child in each one of us just wants to be noticed and loved and accepted exactly as is—not changed or made different.

You can teach,

but you

can't force.

I love children and they love me.

Open, loving communication with children is one of my greatest joys. I listen to what they say, and they listen to what I say. Children always imitate adults. If a child near me is behaving negatively, I examine my own negative beliefs. I know that as I heal myself, I will also help to heal the child. I affirm that I love myself unconditionally. I become consciously willing to let go of all negative beliefs. I become an example of a positive, loving person. The child can then begin to love herself or himself, and their negative behavior dissolves, sometimes immediately, sometimes gradually. I also connect with my own inner child. As I stabilize my adult life, my inner child feels safe and loved. With safety and love comes the willingness to go beyond many old patterns.

I choose to stretch
beyond where I
was when I got up
this morning. I
am ready to
open myself to
something new.

I choose to live my highest awareness.

I choose to remember that every problem has a solution. And to know that this, too, is something I can deal with. Because I choose to look at a situation in this way, the present problem is a temporary thing to me. It is something that I'm working through. I'm a good person. I choose to let go of feeling sorry for myself. I'm willing to learn the lesson and to open up to the good that the Universe has to offer. I choose to be willing to change. I accept the fact that I will not always know how things are to be worked out. I can trust and I can know. Everything is working out for the best. All is well.

With love I see

clearly in every

direction.

I see clearly.

I have clarity of vision and of purpose. My inner knowing always directs me in ways that are for my highest good and greatest joy. I connect with the Infinity of Life where all is perfect, whole, and complete. In the midst of ever-changing life, I am centered. I begin to see the good in everyone and everything.

There is not

something to do.

There is something

to know.

🜚

Communication is a song of love.

Loving communication is one of the happiest and most powerful experiences for people. How do I get to this space? I have done a lot of work on myself, I've read many books, and I've come to understand the principles of life such as, "What I think and say goes out from me, the Universe responds, and it comes back to me." So I begin to ask for help and to observe myself. As I allow myself the space to watch without judgment and without criticism, I begin to make great progress in loving communication. What do I believe? What do I feel? How do I react? How can I love more? And then I say to the Universe, "Teach me to Love."

I am at peace with

the community

of life.

I open my heart to all people.

I think it's time for us to move away from our limited thinking and to develop a more cosmic view of life. The community of human beings on Planet Earth is opening up on a scale that has never been seen before. New levels of spirituality are connecting us. We are learning on a soul level that we are all one. We have chosen to incarnate at this time for a reason. I believe we have chosen on a deep level to be a part of the healing process of the planet. Remember that every time you think a thought, it goes out from you and connects with like-minded people who are thinking the same thing. We can't move to new levels of consciousness if we remain stuck in old judgments, prejudices, guilt, and fears. As we each practice Unconditional Love of ourselves and others, the entire planet will heal.

There has never
been another
person like you
since time began,
so there is nothing
and no one to
compare or
compete with.

I am incomparable!

I am here to learn to love myself and to love other people unconditionally. Even though every person has measurable things about them, such as height and weight, there is far more to me than my physical expression. The immeasurable part of me is where my power is. Comparing myself with other people makes me feel either superior or inferior, never acceptable exactly as I am. What a waste of time and energy. We are all unique, wonderful beings, each different and special. I go within and connect with the unique expression of eternal Oneness that I am and we all are. Everything in the physical world changes. As I flow with these changes, I keep relating to that which is inside me that is deeper than any change.

What we see in

our world is a

mirror of what

we have in

our minds.

My power comes through the use of my mind.

I am Pure Consciousness. I can use this Consciousness in any way I desire. I can choose to be conscious of the realm of lack and limitation, or I can choose to be conscious of the realm of Infinite Oneness, Harmony, and Wholeness. It is One Infinite Consciousness viewed either negatively or positively. At all times I am one with all of life, and I am free to experience love, harmony, beauty, strength, joy, and so much more. I am Consciousness. I am energy. I am safe. I keep learning and growing and changing my consciousness and changing my experience. All is well.

The only thing you
ever have any
control of is your
current thinking.
Your current
thought, the one
you are thinking
now, is totally
under your
control.

I create my own security by trusting the process of life.

If something happens that you feel you have no control over, then affirm a positive statement immediately. Keep saying it over and over to yourself until you move through that little space. When things don't feel right, you might say this to yourself: "All is well, all is well, all is well." Whenever you feel the urge to control things, you could say, "I trust the process of life." During earthquakes or other natural disasters, it may help to say to yourself, "I am in rhythm and harmony with the earth and the movement of the earth." In this way, whatever happens is okay because you are in harmony with the flow of life.

I now recognize

my creativity, and

I honor it.

I create my life each day.

The creativity of the Universe flows through me all day long, and all I have to do to participate in it is to KNOW that I am a part of it. It is easy to recognize creativity when it comes in the form of a painting, a novel, a movie, a new wine, or a new business. Yet I am creating my entire life every moment from the most common, ordinary creation of new cells in my body—from choosing my emotional responses, to my parents and their old patterns, to my present job, my bank account, my relationships with friends, and my very attitudes about myself. One of my most powerful gifts is my imagination. I use it to see good things happening to me and to everyone around me. I am peaceful as I co-create my life with my Higher Self.

The child within is

always worth

healing.

Self-worth and self-esteem are everyone's divine right.

Every act of violence comes from a brutalized child or one that was once taught to hate. We do not condone the violence, but we must find new ways of healing these adults who were brutalized as children. Our current prison systems only teach the inmates to be better criminals. Punishment does not heal. Gang members and murderers are still worthy of our love. They too were once beautiful little babies. Who taught them to treat life the way they do now? I believe prisoners and guards alike need courses in self-esteem and self-worth. We cannot rehabilitate criminals until we heal their minds. The pain they carry and the value systems they have need healing. Let us put love into the prisons and the jails and visualize true healing happening there.

As you learn new
skills, lovingly
support yourself
during the learning
process. Be there
for yourself.

I praise myself for big and little things.

I am a wonderful being. I used to scold and criticize myself because I believed it would help me improve my life, and yet, criticism has not improved me over the years. In fact, criticism seems to make it much harder to change and progress. So, as I listen to my inner dialogue and find that I am being critical, telling myself that I'm not good enough or that I'm doing something wrong, I recognize the old patterns of childhood, and I immediately begin to speak lovingly to my inner child. Instead of tearing myself apart, I choose to nourish myself with praise and approval. I know I am on the way to becoming consistently loving.

Death is a door

opening to a

new life.

I live and die every day.

We all come in during the middle of the movie, and we all leave in the middle of the movie. There is no right time or wrong time, just our time. Death is not a failure. Vegetarians die and meat eaters die. People who curse and people who meditate die. Good people die and bastards die. Everybody goes. It is a normal and natural process. As one door to life closes, another one opens. As the door to this life closes, the door to our next life opens. The love we take with us greets us in our next experience. Death is a releasing method of being born into the next phase of everlasting, eternal life. I know that no matter where I am, I am always safe and loved and totally supported by life.

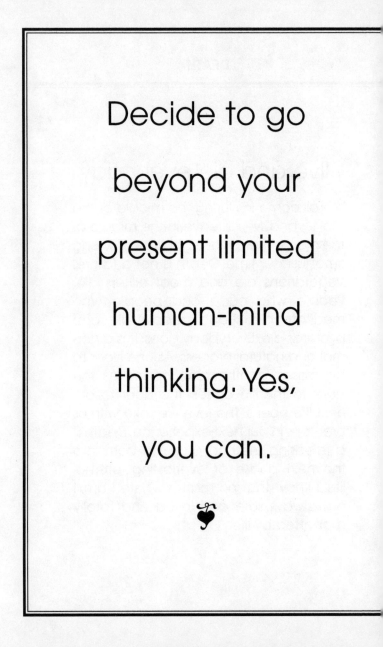

Decide to go
beyond your
present limited
human-mind
thinking. Yes,
you can.

I am a decisive person.

When you care about your physical well-being, you select healthy, nutritious foods to eat. When you care about your mental and emotional well-being, you decide to choose thoughts that create a solid inner foundation for yourself. One idle thought does not mean very much, but thoughts that we think over and over are like drops of water. First there is a puddle, then a pond, then a lake, then an ocean. Repeated criticism and thoughts of lack and limitation drown your consciousness in a sea of negativity, while repeated thoughts of Truth and peace and love lift you up so that you float on the ocean of life with ease. Thoughts that connect you with the Oneness of life make it easier for you to make good decisions and to stick to them.

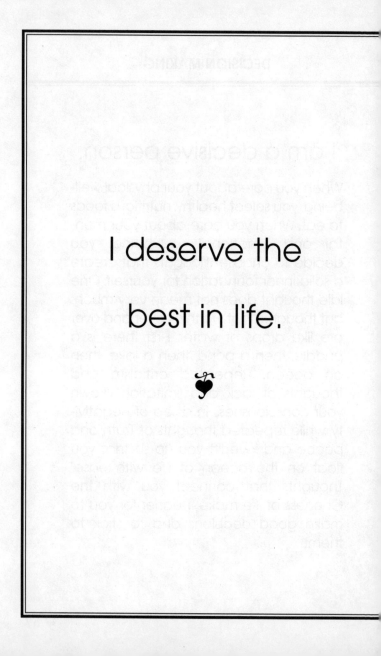

I deserve the

best in life.

I deserve splendid experiences.

All people deserve happy, fulfilling lives. Like most people, I used to believe that I deserved only a little bit of good. Few people believe they deserve ALL GOOD. Do not limit your good. Most of us have been conditioned to believe that the good in life can only be had if you eat your spinach, clean your room, comb your hair, shine your shoes, don't make noise, and so on. Although these may be important things to learn, they have nothing to do with inner self-worth. We need to know that we're already good enough, and that without changing anything at all, we deserve a wonderful life. I open my arms wide and declare with love that I deserve and accept ALL good.

I assimilate the

good in life and

make it true

for me.

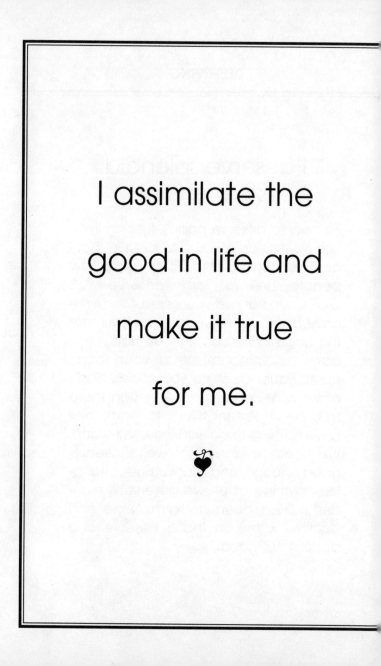

I digest life with ease.

I assimilate, digest, and eliminate life perfectly. My cells and organs know exactly what to do, and I help them do their jobs by doing my job of eating nutritious food and thinking clear, positive, loving thoughts. For every part of my body, there is a mental pattern. The stomach is the part of me where ideas are digested and assimilated. When new experiences happen, I sometimes have problems assimilating them. And yet, even in the midst of a big change, I can always choose the thoughts that glorify my most essential and eternal being. I am a Divine, Magnificent Expression of Life.

I lovingly create

perfect health

for myself.

My dis-ease is a valuable teacher.

It is natural that I am healthy. It is natural that I am flexible, able to learn new things easily, to laugh, to change, and to grow. Dis-ease is related to a resistance to flowing with life in some area, and to the inability to forgive. I look at dis-ease as if it is a personal teacher that comes to help me on my pathway to greater understanding. Like all teachers, it is a stepping stone, and when I learn the lesson, I move on to the next phase of my healing. Every person on the planet is involved in healing their life in some area. I help my body, my mind, and my spirit live healthfully by creating a loving atmosphere around myself. It is my body and my mind, and I am in charge.

I feel good about

what I do.

I flow with life easily and effortlessly.

I flow with an attitude of serendipity through all kinds of experiences. There are endless ways of doing things. If we have done a great deal of work, we rejoice. If we have done very little work, we rejoice. If we have done nothing at all, we still rejoice. Whatever we do is perfect in the moment. There is really nothing that "we have to do." There are things that might be best to do; however, we always have choice. Life is an adventure, and the Universe is always on our side!

When I meditate, I sit down and ask, "What is it I need to know?" At some point during the day, I get an answer.

All is in Divine right Order.

I really know that there is a power far greater than myself that flows through me every moment of every day, and I can open myself to this power and receive what I need, whenever I choose. This is true of everyone. We all are learning that it is safe to look within. It is safe to enlarge our viewpoint of life. If things aren't going the way we expected in some area, it doesn't mean we are bad or wrong. It is a signal that we are being redirected by Divine Guidance. When this happens, find a quiet place where you can relax and connect with the Intelligence within you. Affirm that the supply of wisdom is inexhaustible and available to you, and that whatever you need to know is revealed to you in the perfect time/space sequence.

My dreams are a

joyful, loving

experience.

My bed is a safe place.

Please do not listen to the news or watch it on TV the last thing at night. The news is often a list of disasters, and you don't want to take that into your dream state. Much clearing work is done in dreams. You can also ask your dreams for help with anything you are working on. You will often find an answer by morning. Prepare yourself for sleep by doing something special that helps you calm down. You might use these affirmations: *Every corner of my world is a safe place. Even in the dark of night when I sleep, I am safe. I know tomorrow will take care of itself. My dreams are dreams of joy. I awaken feeling safe and secure. I love waking up. If I awaken with a dream, I ask it to tell me about itself.* Daily practice of your mental skills can begin before you open your eyes. Silently, while still under the covers, give thanks for your cozy bed and all your many blessings.

I love experiencing

every age.

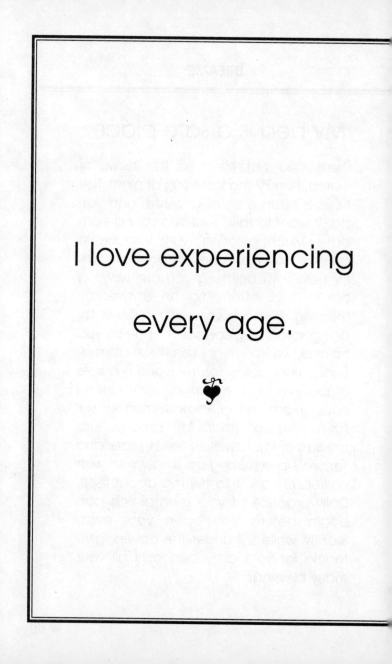

I rejoice in each passing year.

In the early part of this century, the life expectancy was 49 years. Today it is about 85. Tomorrow it could be 125. It is time for us to change the way we view our later years. No longer will we accept the notion that we must become sick and die, lonely and afraid. It is time to make nursing homes obsolete as we learn to take responsibility for our own health. We take control of our thoughts, and we create an elder time that is far grander than any other generation. I see myself as vital, vivacious, healthy, fully alive, and contributing until my last day. I am at peace with my age. As I move into my treasure years, I allow myself to become an Elder of Excellence. I lead the way in showing others how to be fully alive at every age. We each have the ability to contribute to our society and to make the world a better place for our grandchildren.

I do not have to

work hard in order

to deserve a

good income.

I employ positive thoughts.

As I employ my Higher Self, my Higher Self employs me. What a wonderful, brilliant, delicate, strong, beautiful energy my inner spirit is. It blesses me with fulfilling work. Each day is new and different. As I let go of the struggle to survive, I find that I am fed, clothed, housed, and loved in ways that are deeply fulfilling to me. I make it okay for me and others to have money without working hard at a job. I am worthy of bringing in good money without struggling in the rat race or fighting traffic. I follow my higher instincts and listen to my heart in all that I do.

Loving yourself

gives you the

extra energy

needed to work

through any

problems more

quickly.

I am energy.

I liberate my energy by doing things that delight me. As I consciously acknowledge the energy of love in my life, I dissolve old grudges that wear me down. When I feel tired, I rest. I even give myself permission to do absolutely nothing every once in a while. My energy is radiant and peaceful today. Laughing, singing, and dancing are my natural, normal, spontaneous expressions. I know I am part of the Divine plan. I am creating space inside myself for loving, optimistic, and cheerful patterns to constantly germinate, take root, and grow. I nourish them with my positive attitude.

I witness

everything

with love.

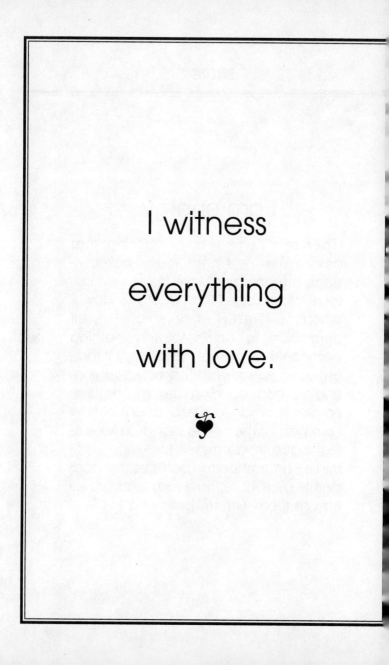

Enlightenment is my 24-hour-a-day job.

Awakening to love is what I am doing each morning. I love stretching my mind and ACTING AS IF I am already Perfect, Whole, and Complete, right here and right now. My heart is open and receptive to all good as I let go of striving and straining to get what I need, and I know everything I need and desire comes to me in the perfect time/space sequence. I feel peaceful knowing that the Universe is on my side. As I align my consciousness with my Higher Self, I flow with an attitude of serendipity through all kinds of experiences.

Bless another
person's good
fortune, and know
that there is
plenty for all.

Other people's prosperity mirrors my own abundance.

My consciousness determines my prosperity. The One Infinite Intelligence always says YES to me, and I say YES to all good. Reverend Ike, the well-known New York City evangelist, remembers walking by good restaurants and lovely homes and fancy automobiles when he was a poor preacher, and saying out loud, "That's for me, that's for me." I rejoice out loud when I see abundance, and I mentally make room for it to come into my life. Being grateful for what I have helps it increase. This also works with talents and abilities and good health. I recognize prosperity everywhere and rejoice in it!

By expanding my

horizons, I easily

dissolve limitations.

Life is free and easy.

How far are we willing to go with expanding the horizons of our thinking? You see, life really is free and easy. It is our thinking that is difficult, limited, shame-based, or not good enough. If we open ourselves to unlearning some of our limited thinking patterns and learning something new, then we can grow and change. Or do we already know it all? The trouble with knowing it all is, you don't get to grow, and nothing new can come in. Do you really accept that there's a Power and an Intelligence greater than you? Or do you think you're the whole thing? See, if you think that you're IT, then, of course, you're frightened. If you realize there's a Power and an Intelligence in this Universe far greater and brighter than you, and which is on your side, then you can move into that mental space where life can operate freely and easily.

Unconditional love is really just love with no expectations.

Just be who you are.

I love myself in this present moment exactly as I am. As I do this, I feel my stomach relax, and I feel the muscles in my neck and back adjust themselves gently. I used to resist loving and accepting myself, believing that I had to wait until I lost the weight or got the job, the lover, the money, or whatever. What happened was when I lost the weight or got the money, I still didn't love myself, and I just made another list. Today, I drop my list of expectations! This moment is incredibly powerful. I am enjoying the feeling of just letting me be who I am.

I picked the

perfect set of

parents for this

lifetime.

All living beings are part of my family.

I envelop my entire family in a circle of love — those who are living, and those who are dead. I affirm wonderful, harmonious experiences that are meaningful for all of us. I feel so blessed to be part of the timeless web of unconditional love that brings us all together. Ancestors who lived before me did the best they could with the knowledge and understanding they had, and children not yet born will face new challenges and will do the best they can with the knowledge and understanding they will have. Each day I see my task more clearly, which is to simply let go of old family limitations and awaken to Divine Harmony. For me, family get-togethers are opportunities to practice tolerance and compassion.

I feel totally safe

everywhere in this

Universe.

I am safe.

At any moment we have the opportunity of choosing love or fear. In moments of fear, I remember the sun. It is always shining even though clouds may obscure it for a while. Like the sun, the One Infinite Power is eternally shining its light upon me, even though clouds of negative thinking may temporarily obscure it. I choose to remember the Light. I feel secure in the Light. And when the fears come, I choose to see them as passing clouds in the sky, and I let them go on their way. I am not my fears. It is safe for me to live without guarding and defending myself all the time. I know that what we do in our hearts is very important, so I begin every day in a silent connection with my heart. When I feel afraid, I open my heart and let the love dissolve the fear.

I cannot be lost

or lonely or

abandoned, for I

dwell in Divine

Intelligence.

❦

There is only one Intelligence.

When I feel lost or when something I need is lost, I stop my panicking thoughts and drop into the Intelligence within me that knows nothing is ever lost in Divine Mind. This Intelligence is everywhere. It is in everything around me. It is in what I am looking for. It is within me Here and Now. I affirm that this One Intelligence is now bringing me and what I'm looking for together in the perfect time/space sequence. I am never stuck. Several times throughout the day, I let go of my limiting identities and remind myself of who I really am — a Divine Magnificent Expression of Life created by a Loving and Infinite Intelligence. All is well.

We create our own
feelings by the
thoughts we choose
to think. We have
the ability to make
different choices
and create different
experiences.

Feelings are thoughts in motion in our bodies.

We can heal what we can feel, so we must allow ourselves to feel our feelings. So many people put judgments on their feelings. They feel they "shouldn't" be angry, but they are. They are searching for a way to deal with their feelings. There are many safe ways to express feelings. You can beat pillows, scream in the car, run, play tennis. You can have a heated conversation in front of a mirror with the people you are angry at or hurt by or afraid of. Imagine these people standing before you. Look in the mirror, and tell them how you really feel. Get it all out, and then finish with something like, "Okay, that's done. I release you and let you go. Now, what do I believe about myself that created this? And what belief could I change so that I will not react with anger all the time?" This is an incredible time to be alive. Be gentle with yourself as you learn your lessons and move through life.

I am financially

comfortable.

I go beyond
the economy.

I allow my income to constantly expand, no matter what the newspapers and economists say. I move beyond my present income, and I go beyond the economic forecasts. I don't listen to people out there telling me how far I can go or what I can do. I easily go beyond my parents' income level. My consciousness of finances is constantly expanding and taking in new ideas — new ways to live deeply, richly, comfortably, and beautifully. My talents and abilities are more than good enough, and it is deeply pleasurable for me to share them with the world. I go beyond any feelings that I do not deserve, and I move into acceptance of a whole new level of financial security.

Love is all I need

to fix my world.

Loving myself is my magic wand.

Every day it gets easier to look into my own eyes in the mirror and say, "I love you just the way you are." My life improves without me fixing it up. I used to be a fix-it person. I'd fix my relationships. I'd fix my bank account. I'd fix things with my boss, my health, and my creativity. Then one day I discovered magic. If I could really love myself, really love every part of me, incredible miracles happened in my life. My problems seemed to dissolve, and there was nothing to fix. So the focus of my attention has changed from fixing problems to loving myself and trusting the Universe to bring to me everything that I need and everything that I desire.

Food is a good
friend. I thank it for
giving its life to
nourish me.

I love eating good food.

Eating good, nutritious food is deeply pleasurable whether I am at home, in a restaurant, camping, hiking, or taking my lunch break at the office. I love myself; therefore, I choose to be aware of what I put into my mouth and how it makes me feel. When I eat, I am putting fuel into my body to give me energy. Every body is different. I can't tell you what to eat because I don't know your body. Find the kind of fuel that your body needs to have optimum health and energy. Fast foods can be fun occasionally, but there are many people who feel it is normal to exist on colas, cakes, and processed convenience foods that have little nutrition in them. Learning about the basics of good nutrition is fun and energizing. I enjoy cooking and eating delicious, healthful, natural food.

Forgiveness is the healing tool I carry with me everywhere.

I am willing to forgive.

I love the feeling of freedom when I take off my heavy coat of criticism, fear, guilt, resentment, and shame. I can then forgive myself and others. This sets us all free. I am willing to give up my stuff around old issues. I refuse to live in the past any longer. I forgive myself for having carried those old burdens for so long. I forgive myself for not knowing how to love myself and others. Each person is responsible for their own behaviors, and what they give out, life will give back to them. So I have no need to punish anyone. We are all under the laws of our own consciousness, myself included. I go about my own business of clearing out the unforgiving parts of my mind, and I allow the love to come in. Then, I am healed.

I make new and
different, more
supportive and
nourishing
choices.

I always have the freedom to choose my thoughts.

No person, place, or thing has any power over me unless I give it, for I am the only thinker in my mind. I have immense freedom in that I can choose what to think. I can choose to see life in positive ways instead of complaining or being mad at myself or other people. Complaining about what I don't have is one way to handle a situation, but it doesn't change anything. When I love myself and I find myself in the midst of a negative situation, I can say something like, "I'm willing to release the pattern in my consciousness that contributed to this condition." We've all made negative choices in the past. Yet, this does not mean we are bad people, nor are we stuck with these negative choices. We can always choose to let go of the old judgments.

I joyously give to

Life, and Life

lovingly gives

to me.

I give and receive gifts graciously.

Appreciation and acceptance act like powerful magnets for miracles every moment of the day. If somebody compliments me, I smile and say thank you. Compliments are gifts of prosperity. I have learned to accept them graciously. Today is a sacred gift from Life. I open my arms wide to receive the full measure of prosperity that the Universe offers this day. Any time of the day or night, I can let it in. I know there are times in life when the Universe gives to me, and I am not in a position to do anything about giving back. I can think of many people who really helped me so much at a time when there was no way I could ever repay them. Later, I've been able to help others, and that's the way life goes. I relax and rejoice in the abundance that is here now.

My goal is to love

myself more

today than

yesterday.

My goal is to be in love with every NOW moment.

I put love into my daily schedule, whether I go to the market or the office or travel around the world or just stay at home. One of our purposes in life is to help heal the world. So we start with healing ourselves. The center of our world is wherever we are. Our thoughts go out from us like ripples in a pond. When we create harmony inside by thinking harmonious thoughts, then that energy goes out from us into the world, touching people and places and things. These vibrations are felt and responded to. Let's make sure that we are radiating harmony and love.

I choose my own

loving concept

of God.

One Power created us all.

I have the power to choose to see things as they really are. I choose to see things as God does, with the eyes of love. Since it is the nature of God to be present everywhere, to be all-powerful and all-knowing, I know that all there really is in this entire Universe is the Love of God. The Love of God surrounds me, indwells me, goes before me, and smoothes the way for me. I am a Beloved Child of the Universe, and the Universe lovingly takes care of me now and forevermore. When I need something, I turn to the Power that created me. I ask for what I need, and then I give thanks even before receiving, knowing that it will come to me in the perfect time/space sequence.

I share only the

good news.

I am an excellent communicator.

Once I became aware of the harm that gossip does to everyone involved with it, I decided to stop gossiping and found that I had nothing to say to anyone for three weeks. So I have learned that it is best if I speak well of my companions. Then, by the law of life, they also speak well of me. In this way, good vibrations accompany me and greet me wherever I go. I like taking the time to be considerate of others, and I absolutely relish communicating in a way that uplifts and inspires people. Knowing that what we give out comes back to us, I carefully choose the words I use. If I hear a negative story, I do not repeat it. If I hear a positive story, I tell everyone.

I value my
freedom, so I
neither give nor
receive guilt.

I love and accept myself exactly as I am.

This is a good affirmation for releasing guilt. As a child, I was manipulated through guilt into good behavior. "Don't be like that," "Don't say that," "No, no, no!" Religion also uses guilt to keep people in line, even telling them that they'll burn in hell if they "misbehave." I forgive the churches and the church authorities. I choose to forgive my parents and to forgive myself. All of us were living under a very heavy mantle of guilt, feeling "not good enough" for whatever reason. This is a new day. Let us take back our power! I start by loving and accepting myself unconditionally.

I am wonderful

just as I am at this

very moment.

I approve of what I see in me.

One of the mental patterns that contributes to headaches is the need to make ourselves wrong. The next time you get a headache, you might ask yourself, "How am I making myself wrong? What have I just done that I'm putting myself down for?" I have learned to listen to my inner dialogue, and when negative thoughts pass through my mind, telling me that I'm not good enough or that I'm doing something wrong, I recognize the old patterns of childhood, and I begin to speak lovingly to myself and my inner child. Instead of tearing myself down with critical thinking, I choose to nourish myself with loving thoughts of approval. If I become aware of something that is pressuring me, I look for ways to handle that pressure differently. I approve of myself.

My body is
peaceful, healthy,
and happy, and
so am I.

Good health is my Divine Right.

I am open and receptive to all the healing energies in the Universe. I know that every cell in my body is intelligent and knows how to heal itself. My body is always working towards perfect health. I now release any and all impediments to my perfect healing. I learn about nutrition and feed my body good, wholesome food. I watch my thinking and only think healthy thoughts. I release, wipe out, and eliminate all thoughts of hatred, jealousy, anger, fear, self-pity, shame, and guilt. I forgive all those who I believe have ever hurt me. I forgive myself for hurting others and for not loving myself more in the past. I love my body. I send love to each organ, bone, muscle, and part of my body. I flood the cells of my body with love. I am grateful to my body for all the good health I have had in the past. I accept healing and good health here and now.

Loving myself and

others allows me

to be all that I

can be.

I always work for my highest good.

The power that created me is the same power that I co-create with, and this power only wants me to express and experience my highest good. I do my best to make my Real Self vitally important and give it control of everything. By doing this, I am truly Loving my Self. It opens me to greater possibilities, to freedom, joy, and unpredictably wonderful daily miracles. My Highest Good includes the highest good for others, too. This is truly a loving act.

Holidays are

happy times

for me.

Every day is a holy day.

Religious and civic holidays are times to celebrate with friends and reflect upon the processes of life. I follow my inner voice through each holiday, always knowing that I am in the right place, at the right time, doing the right thing for me. I have fun at parties and holiday get-togethers. I know how to have a good time and be responsible and safe all in the same evening. There is time for laughter and time for being grateful for my many blessings. I connect with my inner child, and we do something together, just the two of us. When I go shopping for holiday gifts, I easily purchase what I need at prices I can afford. Everyone welcomes the gifts I give.

My inner home
and my outer
home are places
of beauty and
peace.

My heart is my home.

I am at home in my own heart. I take my heart with me to wherever I live. As we begin to love ourselves, we find ourselves providing a safe and comfortable home for ourselves. We begin to feel at home in our own bodies. Our homes are reflections of our minds and what we feel we are worthy of. If your home is a disaster zone and you feel overwhelmed, then just begin with one corner of one of the rooms. Just like with your mind, begin with changing one thought at a time. Eventually, the whole place will be tidy. As you work, remind yourself that you are also cleaning the rooms of your mind.

I continually clean

the rooms of

my mind.

Simple household chores are a snap for me.

I make housework fun. I begin anywhere and move through the rooms with artistic flair. I toss out the garbage. I dust and polish those things I treasure. We all have a set of beliefs. And just like a comfortable, familiar reading chair, we keep sitting in these beliefs over and over and over again. Our beliefs create our experiences. Some of these beliefs create wonderful experiences. And some of them can become like an uncomfortable old chair that we don't want to throw out. I know that I really can toss out old beliefs, and I can choose new ones that significantly improve the quality of my life. It's like housecleaning. I need to clean my physical house periodically, otherwise it gets to a point where I really can't live in it. I don't have to be fanatical. I do need to clean. Physically and mentally, I fill the rooms of my house with love.

I love

to laugh.

I use my humor wisely.

The subconscious mind has no sense of humor. If I make a joke about myself or put myself down and just think, Oh, it doesn't mean anything, I'm only kidding myself, my subconscious mind accepts it as true and creates accordingly. If I tell put-downs or ethnic-slur jokes about others, I am still under the law of "what I give out will come back to me." So I have learned to use my humor lovingly and wisely. There is so much humor in life that it is not necessary to denigrate another person or group. Even in humor we are working to help make the world a more loving and safer place to live.

I share my

resources and my

knowledge with

all of life.

Everything we need is here.

I see old doors closing on hunger, poverty, and suffering; and I see new doors opening on the just distribution of all resources. There is an incredible abundance on this planet and literally enough food to feed everyone. Yet people are starving. The problem is not a lack of food. It is a lack of love. It is a consciousness that believes in lack, plus people who feel that they don't deserve good in their lives. We must help to raise the consciousness of all people on the planet. To feed someone once is good, and they will be hungry again tomorrow. To teach a person how to fish will enable them to feed themselves for the rest of their lives.

My thoughts

support and

strengthen my

immune system.

My body is intelligent.

Every day it is getting easier and easier to give myself a good dose of Unconditional Love. I believe that what I "pick up" depends on where I am in consciousness. Do I believe that "life is hard and I always get the short end of the stick," or "I'm no good anyway, so what difference does it make"? If my beliefs run along these lines, then my immune system (which registers my thoughts and feelings) will be lowered and open to whatever "bug" or "germ" is around at the time. However, if I believe that "life is a joy, and I am lovable and my needs are always met," then my immune system will feel supported, and my body will more easily fight off dis-ease.

Inner work always
improves the
quality of
our lives.

Every day I listen for one new idea that will improve the quality of my life.

I am a simple human being with an amazingly complex structure of beliefs. I am learning how to get to the love behind the appearances in each of my personal issues. I am kind and patient with myself as I learn and grow and change. Life seems to flow much easier when I make peace with myself on an inner level. It's important to know I can make changes without seeing myself as a bad person. For too long I have felt I had to be wrong or bad in order to make a change. I thought it was essential in order to make a change, but it isn't. It just makes changing very difficult. When I come from loving acceptance, then the positive changes I desire come to me so much easier. Improvement, after all, is natural.

My increasing

financial status

reflects my

changing beliefs

about income.

I bless my income with love and watch it grow.

My income is perfect for me. Every day I love myself a little more, and as I do, I find that I am open to new avenues of income. Prosperity comes through many forms and channels. It is not limited. Some people limit their incomes by saying that they live on a fixed income. But who fixed it? Some people feel that they don't deserve to earn more than their father earned or to go beyond their parents' worthiness level. Well, I can love my parents and still go beyond their income level. There is One Infinite Universe, and out of it comes all the income that everyone makes. The income I am presently making reflects my beliefs and my deservability. It has nothing to do with getting. It's really allowing myself to accept. I accept a healthy flow of income for myself.

I am an individual

expression of Life.

I am a light in the world.

I follow my inner star and sparkle and shine in my own unique way. I am a very precious Being. I have a beautiful soul, and I have an outer body and a personality. But my soul is the center. My soul is the part of me that is eternal. It always has been and always will be. My soul has taken on many personalities. And will take on many more. My soul cannot be hurt or destroyed. It can only be enriched by whatever the life experiences are. There is so much more to life than I can comprehend. I shall never know all the answers. But the more I allow myself to understand how life works, the more of the power and force I have available to use.

I have made

lessons easy

and fun.

I am willing to learn.

I am learning to look for the love that is always hidden inside every lesson. Each one of us is here to learn lessons. I am learning about the relationship between my thoughts and my experiences, and I am doing the best I can with the knowledge and understanding I have. Learning "the lesson" has to do with being willing to change. My Higher, Spiritual Self is changeless and eternal, and so all that really changes is my temporary, human self. I have been taught to believe it is hard to change. Well, I now know that I can choose to buy into that, or I can choose to believe it is easy to change. I can resist, deny, get angry, and build walls, but eventually I will learn the lesson anyway. It helps to be willing to learn.

New, wonderful
experiences now
enter my life.
I am safe.

I pay attention to the good in life.

I know that good resides in every moment and in every place, and that even in the worst situation, a bit of goodness can be found. The loss of a job or a loved one or my health brings me face to face with my biggest fears. It is normal and natural that I experience these fears. Yet I know that nature abhors a vacuum. When one thing goes, then something else will come to take its place. So I take a deep breath—or six— and trust life to always take care of all my needs. I am learning to trust. Life loves me and will never let me down. Only that which is for my highest good now occurs.

I rejoice in the
love I have to
share.

I am a radiant being of love.

Deep at the center of my being there is an infinite supply of love. It is inexhaustible. I can never use it all in this lifetime. So I don't have to be sparing with it. I can always be generous with my love. Love is contagious. When I share love, it comes back to me multiplied. The more love I give, the more love I have. I have come to this world to be a love giver. I came in full of love. And even though I will share my love all my life, when I leave this earth I will still have a full and happy heart. If I want more love, then I have only to give love. Love is and I am.

I am wisely
guided in all my
financial affairs.

Conscious prosperity benefits all.

I rejoice that I am at a point in life where I can make a major purchase. While it is natural for me to carry a peaceful feeling with me when I go shopping, at this point I feel excited. When there is a lot of money involved, I open my heart and let love flow into all aspects of the transaction. Purchasing a large appliance, a car, or even a home is a smooth operation for me, as well as for the salespeople, bankers, accountants, and everyone else involved. The paperwork is in perfect order. I rejoice that it is natural for me to wisely handle larger amounts of my own money. I stay in the present moment as I follow my heart and let abundance flow through every cell in my body.

My Higher Self

is immune to

manipulation

and guilt.

My Higher Self pilots my life.

I am not here to please other people or to live my life their way. I am here to learn how to love myself and to love other people unconditionally. No one can manipulate me without my consent. When I don't know who I am, I am prone to being what someone else wants me to be; therefore, I am interested in learning to know myself. I know that I do not have to fit into anyone else's emotional atmosphere. Nor do I have to manipulate others to fit them into my emotional atmosphere. When manipulative games are going on, it is important to connect with the little child within me and reassure it that I love it and that together we are going to get through this. I call upon my Higher Self now and accept its love and wisdom.

I cherish my

meditation times.

The wisdom I seek is within me.

At least once a day I sit quietly and go within to connect with the wisdom and knowledge that is always there. This wisdom and knowledge is only a breath away. All the answers to all the questions I shall ever ask are sitting there waiting for me. Meditating is a joy for me. I sit quietly, take a few deep breaths, relax, and go to that place of peace within. After a little while, I come back to the present moment refreshed and renewed and ready for life. Every day is a joyous new adventure for me because I choose to listen to my own inner wisdom. This wisdom is always available to me. It comes from the essence of that which exists behind the universe of time, space, and change. When I meditate, I connect with the deep inner unchanging part of myself. Here I am energy. I am light. I am the answer already arrived. I am eternal Beingness being here now.

In the area of

finances, I am

always prosperous.

Money loves me and comes to me like a beloved puppy.

Money is merely a means of exchange. It is a form of giving and receiving. As I give to life, life gives to me abundance in all its many forms, including money. I am always financially secure. Money that comes to me is a pleasure to handle. I save some and spend some. I eliminate thoughts of indebtedness, guilt, and any other negative, poverty-oriented thinking. I always have enough money. Establishing credit is easy for me. I pay my bills with love and acknowledge my true Source.

Money can be

one of my

best friends.

Money is one of the easiest things to demonstrate.

That statement usually makes us feel angry. Especially if we're having money worries. Our beliefs about money are so ingrained that it's hard to talk about them without a lot of emotion coming up. It's much easier to teach a workshop on sex than on money. We get very angry when our money patterns are challenged. Be aware of how you really feel about money. You could look into a mirror and say to yourself, "My biggest worry with respect to money is____," and then relax and let the feelings come up. Maybe you'll hear: "I can't take care of myself," or "I'll turn out poor just like Dad," or "I'll starve and become a bag lady," or "I just don't trust myself." Listen what comes, and write it down. You might find yourself saying: "Wow, look at what I believe! No wonder I'm not having the prosperity I want." Become aware of what belief is blocking the flow of money. Then begin to change the beliefs. Instead of running the thought that, "I'm going to starve," I can begin to love myself with new thoughts such as, "I'm safe in the Universe. Everything I need is provided. I now allow myself to earn a good income."

🍂 151

I am at peace

with my loved

one's passing.

I am at peace with the grieving process.

The mourning process takes at least a year. I have to experience the special holidays I shared with this person. I give myself time and space to go through this natural, normal process of life. I am gentle with myself. I just allow myself to go through the grief. After a year, it begins to dissipate. I am aware that I can never lose anyone because I have never owned anyone. And in what will seem like a twinkling of an eye, I will connect with that soul again. I feel surrounded by love now, and I surround them with love wherever they are. Everybody dies. Trees, animals, birds, rivers, and even stars are born and die, and so do I. And all in the perfect time-space sequence.

Every moment is a

new beginning

point.

I enjoy new ways of thinking.

We do a lot of vacillating between old ideas and new ways of thinking. Be patient with yourself through this process. Beating yourself up only keeps you stuck. It's better to build yourself up instead. Anything you say or think is an affirmation. Really be aware of your thoughts and your words; you might discover that a lot of them are very negative. Many people tend to approach life through negative eyes. They take an ordinary situation like a rainy day and say something like, "Oh what a terrible day." It isn't a terrible day. It's a wet day. To create a wonderful day sometimes takes just a slight change in the way you look at it. Be willing to let go of an old, negative way that you look at something, and look at it in a new, positive way.

I spread the

good news.

I envision positive news reports.

We read so much in the news about disasters; there is so much bad news flooding our consciousness. If you read and listen to the news all the time, you are sure to scare yourself. I gave up reading the newspapers a long time ago. Any piece of news I am meant to know, someone will tell me. The media wants to sell their products, and they dig up the worst scenarios to catch our attention. I would like to see a boycott on all news until the media begins to tell us at least 75 percent good news. This would encourage us all to see life in a more positive way. We could begin by writing to the papers and magazines and TV stations and requesting more good news. Together, we can envision positive news happening, and we can hear the cry for love that is hidden in every negative report.

I lovingly take

charge of my

body now.

I nourish myself with love.

I care enough for myself to nourish myself with all the best that Life has to offer. I learn about nutrition because I am a precious being, and I want to take the best care of me that I can. My body is special and different from all other bodies; therefore, I learn the things that my body assimilates the best. I learn everything I can about food and beverages. I pay attention to what I eat and drink, and I notice if some food or beverage does not seem to agree with me. If I have something to eat and an hour later I fall asleep, I realize that that particular food is not good for my body at this time. I search out the foods that give me good energy. I bless all my food with love and gratitude. I am nurtured and nourished. I feel healthy, happy, and great.

I choose the thoughts that make me feel comfortable with growing older.

❧

I am the perfect age.

Each year is special and precious and filled with wonders all its own. Being elderly is as special as being a child. Yet, my culture fears old age so much. We've made it such a terrible, terrible thing to get old. And yet it's normal and natural. We've created a youth-worship culture that is harmful to us all. I look forward to growing older. The alternative is to leave the planet. I choose to love myself at every age. Just because I am older it does not mean I have to get sick and infirm. I do not have to be hooked up to machines or suffer in nursing homes in order to leave the planet. When it's my time to go, I'll do it gently—perhaps go to bed, take a nap, and leave peacefully.

Have your mother

make a tape

telling you how

wonderful you are.

I live in the Now.

Old tapes of my childhood used to run my life. Most people have about 25,000 hours of parent tapes running through them. Many of these old tapes had a lot of negative messages in them, lots of criticism and "shoulds." Now I am choosing to erase and retape new positive messages. I listen to my inner thoughts, and when I catch one that makes me feel uncomfortable, I turn it around. So, retape the old messages. You don't have to obediently listen to the old stuff. Just retape. I know I am a capable person. I know I am worth loving. I really believe I am worthy of a wonderful life. I have a purpose in being here. I have the power to change the tapes. Those old, negative messages are not the truth of my Being.

I am a neat and

orderly person.

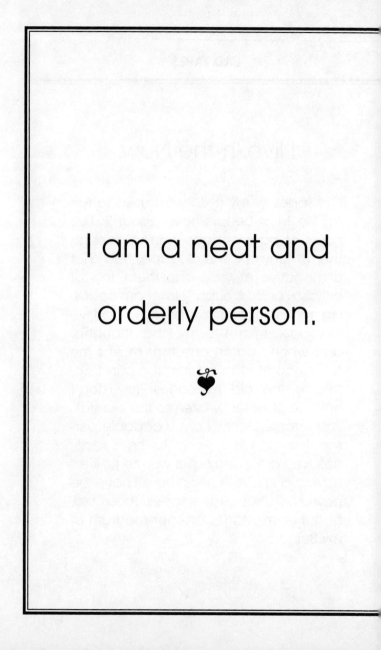

Everything I need is at hand.

It gives me pleasure to arrange my things in such a way that when I am looking for them I can easily find them. Everything is in Divine Right Order, from the stars in the heavens to the clothes in my closet and the papers in my desk. I love the ceremony of my daily routines that exercise my body and train my mind. It seems that when my life is in order, I have the time to be creative and open to new insights. And still, my routines are flexible and fun and effective in helping me do what I came here to do. I am part of the Divine plan. All is in perfect order.

Love will always

dissolve pain.

I replace punishing thoughts with forgiving thoughts.

My Higher Self shows me the way to live a pain-free life. I am learning to respond to pain as if it were an alarm clock signaling me to wake up to my inner wisdom. If I have pain, I start right away with my mental work. I often replace the word "pain" with the word "sensation." My body is having a lot of "sensation." This little shift in words helps me focus my consciousness on healing, which helps me heal much quicker. I know that as I alter my mind just a little bit, my body is altered in a similar direction. I love my body, and I love my mind, and I am thankful that they are so closely related.

Parents are

wonderful

people.

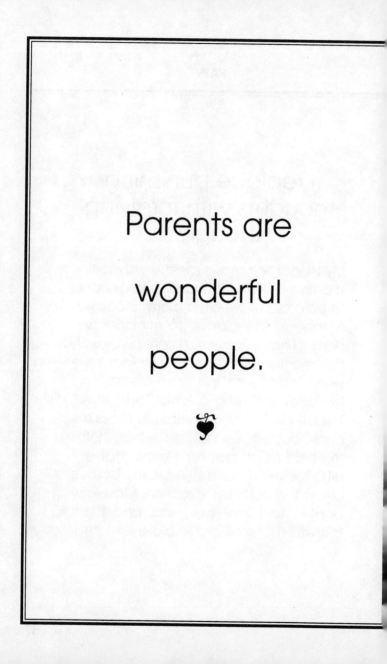

They, too, were children once.

Now is the time for me to stand up on my own two feet, to support myself, to think for myself. To give myself what my parents couldn't give me. The more I learn about their childhoods, the more I understand their limitations. No one taught them how to be parents. They were living out the limitations of their own parents. Parent issues are something we all deal with every day. So the best we can do is to love them as they are and affirm that they love us as we are. I do not use my parents as an excuse for the negative parts of my life. I bless my parents with love and release them to happiness that is meaningful to them.

All is well.

I have everything

I need now.

I have plenty of time.

When I am impatient, I know it is because I do not want to take the time to learn the lesson at hand. I want it done now. Or as I once heard: "Instant gratification is not soon enough." There is always something to learn, something to know. Patience is being at peace with the process of life, knowing that everything happens in the perfect time/space sequence. If I am not having completion now, then there is something more for me to know or do. Being impatient does not speed up the process; it only wastes time. So I breathe, go within, and ask, "What is it I need to know?" Then I patiently wait to receive the help that is all around me.

I choose a

peaceful way

of life.

Peace begins with me.

If I want to live in a peaceful world, then it is up to me to make sure I am a peaceful person. No matter how others behave, I keep peace in my heart. I declare peace in the midst of chaos or madness. I surround all difficult situations with peace and love. I send thoughts of peace to all troubled parts of the world. If I want the world to change for the better, then I need to change the way I see the world. I am now willing to see life in a very positive way. I know that peace begins with my own thoughts. As I continue to have peaceful thoughts, I am connected with like-minded peaceful-thinking people. Together we will help bring peace and plenty to our world.

My life is in order

at a very

deep level.

The Universe is in perfect order.

The stars, the moon, and the sun are all operating in perfect divine right order. There is an order, a rhythm, and a purpose to their pathways. I am part of the Universe; therefore, I know that there is an order, a rhythm, and a purpose to my life. Sometimes my life may seem to be in chaos, and yet in back of the chaos I know there is a divine order. As I put my mind in order and learn my lessons, the chaos disappears, and then order comes back. I trust that my life is really in perfect divine right order. All is well in my world.

We are wonderful

spiritual beings

having a human

experience.

I am perfect, whole, and complete.

No little baby ever says, "Oh, my hips are too big," or "My nose is too long." They know how perfect they are, and once we were all like that. We accepted our perfection as normal and natural. As we grew up we began to doubt our perfection, and we tried to become perfect. We cannot become what we already are. We can only accept it. And so we created stress and strain. There is nothing wrong with any of us. So let's once again affirm and know that we are Divine, Magnificent Expressions of Life and that, really, all is well in our world.

I see the planet

healed and

whole, with

everyone fed,

clothed, housed,

and happy.

I affirm positive solutions for the highest good of all concerned.

There is so much good I can do for the planet on an individual level. At times I may work for causes, putting my physical energy or finances into them. And at other times I may use the power of my thoughts to help heal the planet. If I hear news of a world disaster or acts of senseless violence, I use my mind in a positive way. I know that if I send angry thoughts towards those responsible, then I am not helping to heal. So I immediately surround the whole situation with love and affirm that out of this experience only good will come. I send positive energy and do visualizations, seeing the incident working out as quickly as possible with a solution that is for the best for everyone. I bless the perpetrators with love and affirm that the part of them where love and compassion dwells comes to the surface and that they too are healed. It is only when we are all healed and whole that we will have a healing world to live in.

I love the planet.

I appreciate the beautiful world I live in.

The earth is a wise and loving mother. She provides everything we could ever want. All our needs are taken care of. There is water, food, air, and companionship. We have an infinite variety of animals, vegetation, birds, fish, and incredible beauty. We have treated this planet very badly in the last few years. We have been using up our valuable resources. If we continue to wastefully trash the planet, we will have no place to live. I have committed to lovingly take care of and improve the quality of life in this world. My thoughts are clear and loving and concerned. I express random acts of kindness whenever I can. I recycle and compost and organically garden and improve the quality of the soil. It is my planet, and I help to make it a better place to live. I spend quiet time every day actively imagining a peaceful planet. I imagine the possibilities of a clean, healthy environment. I envision the governments of the world working together to balance their budgets and handle money fairly. I see all the people on the planet opening their hearts and their minds and working together to create a world where it is safe for us to love each other. It is possible. And it starts with me.

The point of
power is in the
present moment.
Claim your Power.

I accept my power.

You have the power to heal your life, and you need to know that. We think so often that we are helpless, but we're not. We always have the power of our minds. Do you use your mind to think of yourself as a victim? Do you walk around feeling mad at yourself, or complaining about others? Do you feel as though you have no power to do anything about changing your life? This is giving your power away. Your mind is a powerful tool. Claim and consciously use your power. You have the power to choose to see things working out for the best. Recognize that you are always connected with the One Power and Intelligence that created you. Feel and use this support. It is there.

We are all one.

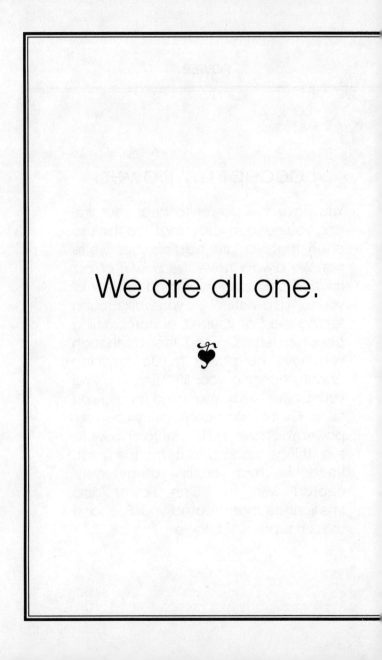

Love is deeper than differences.

The new energy on the planet is loving. I spend time every day opening my mind and my heart to feel a kinship with all people. No matter where I was born or raised, no matter what color skin I have or what religion I was raised to believe in, everything and everyone is plugged into the One Power, and through it all, our needs are met. I have warm, loving, open communication with every member of my earthly family. There are those who look at life so differently; there are the younger ones, older ones, gay ones, straight ones, different-colored ones. I am a member of earth's community. Differences of opinion are wonderful, colorful varieties of expression, not reason to take sides or go to war. As I dissolve prejudice in myself, the whole planet is blessed. Today my heart opens a little more as I go about the work of creating a world where it is safe for us to love each other.

I have a

prosperous

consciousness.

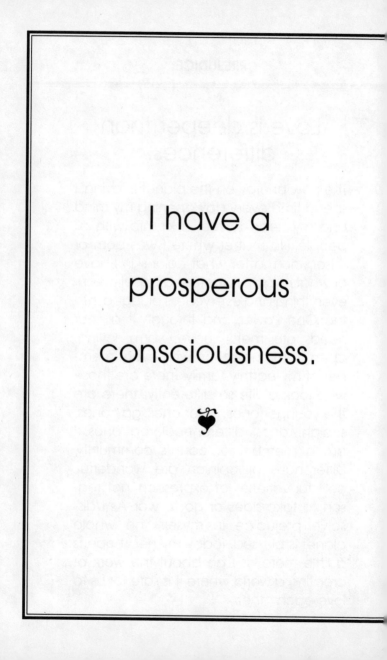

I always have everything I need.

I have inherited a great treasure—the love in my own heart. The more I share this treasure with others, the richer I become. Prosperity begins with feeling good about myself. It doesn't matter how much money I have. If I don't feel good about myself, I can't really enjoy any amount of money. My home, car, clothing, friends, and bank account are only reflections of my thoughts about myself, and no matter where I am or what is happening, I can change my thoughts. True prosperity is never an amount of money; it is a state of mind. My mind is open to receiving prosperity. Once a day, I stretch my arms out wide to the side and say, "I am open and receptive to all the good and abundance in the Universe."

I am here to serve

a purpose.

My purpose is to learn to love unconditionally.

Being alive at this time is an incredible opportunity to explore and experience the Universe and myself. In a way, the self is the new frontier. I've come to know my limited self pretty well, and now I am coming to know my Unlimited Self. My purpose is unfolding through each moment as I calm down and center myself in knowing that I am far more than my personality, problems, fears, or dis-eases. I am spirit, light, energy, and love, and I have the power to live my life with purpose and meaning. And even if I don't think I'm doing it as well as I could do it, I know I'm still doing it well. I love myself, and I am so grateful to be here.

All my experiences

are part of the

richness and

fullness of my life.

I accept all of me.

Life is sacred. I hold to my heart all the parts of myself — the infant, the child, the teenager, young adult, adult, and future self. Every embarrassment, mistake, hurt, and wound, I accept fully as part of my story. My story includes every success and every failure, every error and every truthful insight, and all of it is valuable in ways I don't have to figure out. Sometimes the painful parts of my story help other people understand their own pain. When other people share their pain with me, I feel compassion for them. I now extend this same compassion to myself. I relax in knowing everything about me is acceptable.

My best relationship

is the one I have

with me.

I'm creating lots of room for love.

Relationships are wonderful, and marriages are wonderful, but they're all temporary because there comes a time when they end. The one person I am with forever is me. My relationship with me is eternal. So I am my own best friend. I spend a little time each day connecting with my heart. I quiet down and feel my own love flowing through my body, dissolving fears and guilt. I literally feel love soaking into every cell in my body. I know that I am always connected to a Universe that loves me and everyone else unconditionally. This unconditionally loving Universe is the Power that created me, and it is always here for me. As I create a safe place in myself for love, I draw to me loving people and loving experiences. It is time to let go of my stuff about how relationships are supposed to be.

All my new habits

support me in

positive ways.

I release the need to be perfect.

When I am ready to let an old pattern go, it comes up as an issue. I am learning to recognize my issues as messengers from a deep place inside myself that yearns to be loved. I ask the Universe to help me let go of the fear, and I allow myself to move into the new understanding. I am learning to be loving to my negative habits and beliefs. I used to say, "Oh, I want to get rid of that." Now I know that I created all my habits to fulfill a purpose. So I release the old habits with love and find more positive ways to fulfill those needs.

My religion is

based on love.

I connect with the Power that created me.

I am steady and secure as I connect with the One Infinite Intelligence, the Eternal Power that created me and everything else in existence throughout the Universe. I feel this power within me. Every nerve and cell in my body recognizes this power as good. The reality of my Being is always connected with the Power that created me regardless of what any religion tells me. The savior of my life is within me. As I accept myself and know that I am good enough, I open myself to the healing power of my own love. The love of the Universe surrounds me and indwells me. I am worthy of this love. Love is now flowing through my life. Find a concept of God that supports you.

I release and
I forgive.

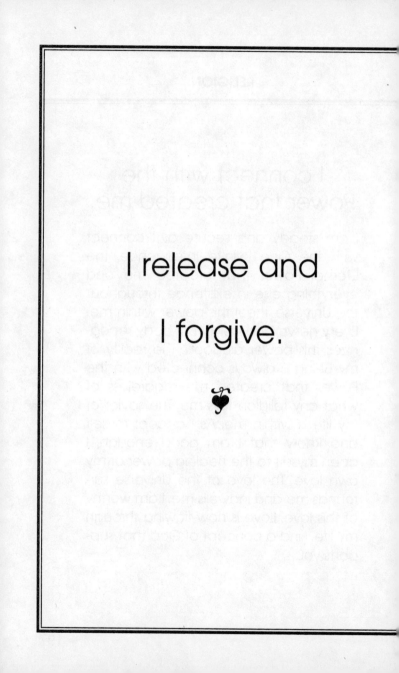

I release the need to dwell in resentment.

Babies express their anger freely. As we grow up, we learn to stuff our anger, and it turns into resentment. It lodges in our bodies, eating away at us. In years past, like many people, I used to live in a prison of self-righteous resentment. I felt I had the right to be angry because of all the things "they" did to me. It took me a long time to learn that holding on to bitterness and resentment did me more harm than the original incident. When I refused to forgive, I was the person who was hurting. The door to my heart was sealed, and I could not love. I learned that forgiveness did not mean that I condoned another person's negative behavior. Releasing my resentment let me out of prison. The door to my heart opened, and I found that I was free. I forgive, I let go, and I fly free.

I am the responsible

power in my life.

I accept my responsibilities with flair.

When we first hear that we are responsible for our experiences, we think we are being blamed. And blame makes us feel guilty and wrong. However, there is no blame involved. To understand that we are responsible is to be given a great gift. For the same power that helps to create experiences can also change them. We go from being powerless over our circumstances to being people who can mold and shape our lives in positive ways. As we learn to use our thoughts in productive ways, we become powerful people. It gives us the power to respond to life, to make changes, and improve the quality of our lives.

I have good

self-esteem, and

I am safe.

I love myself enough to refuse to have sex that is not safe.

Women have had the complete burden of safe sex for hundreds, if not thousands, of years. If women did not practice safe sex, then they were open to the current infectious diseases, as well as to getting pregnant. Now, men, particularly gay men, are also beginning to understand what this experience is like. When the body is in the heat of passion, it does not want to listen to the mind giving it careful instructions on safety. What do you say to someone who refuses to wear a condom? The answer always has to do with your own level of self-esteem. If your self-love and self-esteem are high, you will refuse to have sex that is not safe. If you don't think much of yourself, you will probably "give in" and hope it will be all right. How much do you love yourself? How much will you allow yourself to be abused? Less and less, as your love for yourself grows. People who love themselves will not abuse themselves or others.

Love makes my

world go round.

My love is powerful.

I treat myself as if I am someone who is deeply loved. All kinds of events come and go; yet, through it all, the love for myself is constant. This is not being vain or conceited. People who are vain or conceited have a lot of self-hatred covered over by a layer of "I'm better than you." Self-love is simply appreciating the miracle of my own Being. When I really love myself, I cannot hurt myself, and I cannot hurt another person. To me, the answer to world peace is unconditional love. It begins with self-acceptance and self-love. I no longer wait to be perfect in order to love myself. I accept myself exactly as I am right here and now.

I love my own

thoughts.

My inner dialogue is kind and loving.

I have a unique role to play on this earth, and I also have the tools to do the job. The thoughts I think and the words I speak are my incredibly powerful tools. I use them and I enjoy what they produce for me! Meditation, prayer, or ten minutes of affirmations in the morning are wonderful. And I get better results when I am consistent all day long. I remember that it's the moment-to-moment thinking that is really shaping my life. The point of power, the place where I make changes, is always right here and now. So, just for a moment, I catch the thought I'm thinking right now. And I ask myself, do I want that thought to create my future?

I am the perfect

me, physically,

sexually, mentally,

and spiritually.

I am at peace with my sexuality.

I believe that each lifetime before we are born we choose our country, our color, our sexuality, and the perfect set of parents to match the patterns we have chosen to work on in this lifetime. Each lifetime I seem to choose a different sexuality. Sometimes I am a man, sometimes I am a woman. Sometimes I am heterosexual, sometimes I am homosexual. Each form of sexuality has its own areas of fulfillment and challenges. Sometimes society approves of my sexuality, and sometimes it does not. Yet at all times I am me—perfect, whole, and complete. My soul has no sexuality. It is only my personality that has sexuality. I love and cherish every part of my body including my genitals.

When we are
ready to grow, it
will unfold in
wondrous ways.

I am willing to change.

My spiritual growth often comes to me in strange ways. It can be a chance meeting or an accident, a dis-ease or the loss of a loved one. Something inside urges me to follow, or I am forcefully prevented from living in the same old way. It is a little different for each person. I grow spiritually when I accept responsibility for my life. This gives me the inner power to make the changes in myself that I need to make. Spiritual growth is not about changing others. Spiritual growth happens to the person who is ready to step out of the victim role, into forgiveness, and into a new life. None of this happens overnight. It is an unfolding process. Loving myself opens the door, and being willing to change really helps.

You cannot bend Spiritual Laws to your old way of thinking. You must learn and follow the new language, and when you do, then "magic" will be demonstrated in your life.

The Laws of Energy are always operating.

I am protected by the best insurance plan under the sun: knowledge of Universal Laws and a love of working with them in all areas of my life. Learning Spiritual Laws is very much like learning to operate a computer or VCR. When I calm down and slowly and patiently learn the step-by-step procedures of the computer, it works beautifully. It is almost like magic. If I don't do my homework and don't follow the computer's laws to the letter, then either nothing happens or it won't work the way I want it to work. The computer does not give an inch. I can get as frustrated as I want while it patiently waits for me to learn its laws, and then it gives me magic. It takes practice. And it is the same with learning the Spiritual Laws.

I consciously

connect with my

subconscious

mind.

I program my subconscious mind with loving messages.

My subconscious mind is a storehouse of information. It records everything I think and say. If I put negative in, then I get negative out. When I put positive in, I get positive out. Therefore, I consciously choose to feed it positive, loving, and uplifting messages that produce beneficial experiences for me. I now release any thought, idea, or belief that limits me. I reprogram my subconscious mind with new beliefs that create the most wonderful, prosperous, joyous events in my life.

To succeed, you must believe the thought that you are a success, rather than the thought that you are a failure.

My every perception is a success.

I have within me all the ingredients for success, just like the acorn has the complete oak tree curled within its tiny form. I set standards that are achievable for where I am right now. I encourage and praise my improvements. It's okay for me to learn from every experience, and it's okay for me to make mistakes while I'm learning. This is the way I move from success to success, and every day it gets a little easier to see things in this light. When failure appears before me, I no longer run away from it; rather, I acknowledge it as a lesson. I give failure no power. There is only One Power in this entire Universe, and this Power is 100 percent successful in everything it does. It created me; therefore, I am already a beautiful, successful person.

I relax, knowing

that Life supports

me at all times.

I am supported by Life.

I am neither lonely nor abandoned in the Universe. All of Life supports me every moment of the day and night. Everything I need for a fulfilling life is already provided for me. There is enough breath to last me for as long as I shall live. The earth is supplied with an abundance of food. There are millions of people to interact with. I am supported in every possible way. Every thought I think is mirrored for me in my experiences. Life always says "Yes" to me. All I need do is accept this abundance and support with joy and pleasure and gratitude. I now release from within my consciousness any and all patterns or beliefs that would deny me my good. I am loved and supported by Life itself.

We make

quantum leaps

in consciousness

together.

There is help wherever I turn.

The new social norm is "support groups." There are support groups for any problem we as individuals may have. We have self-help groups, personal growth groups, spiritual growth groups, and 12 Step Programs. These support groups are much more beneficial than sitting around in bars together. We learn we do not have to struggle to figure it all out by ourselves. We do not have to stay stuck in our patterns. We can reach out to a group of like-minded people who have the same problems that we have, and we can work together to find positive solutions. We care for and support each other, knowing that as we do so we learn to leave the pain of the past behind. We do not sit in self-pity bemoaning our past and playing "Ain't it awful." We look for ways to forgive and get on with our lives. As I support you, you support me, and we heal together.

My doctors are
pleased that I am
healing so quickly.

It is safe for me to get well.

Whenever I need a doctor or health care professional, I always choose one with healing hands, a positive attitude, and a loving heart. My decisions for treatment are respected, and I really feel that I am a part of the healing team. I know the real healing power is within me, and I trust it to guide me on my journey. As I quiet down and focus on the beautiful things in my life, I create an atmosphere around me of love and understanding. I know that the wisdom of the Universe works through the medical profession, so I relax and accept its gentle, caring attention as I move through this experience. Every hand that touches my body is a healing hand.

My thoughts

contribute to

my safety.

I gently focus my mind upon the beautiful things in life.

I walk upon this planet safe and secure, knowing that I am always connected with an unlimited and benevolent Universe. In the dark of the night, I used to hear scary sounds. I was afraid of the unknown. In the dark of my mind, I used to think scary thoughts. I would replay long-gone terrors from childhood. I would cringe from imagined accidents. Yet, in this present moment, I can choose to let go of these terrors and to use my mind to think of good things happening. I select a positive, vivid image that is meaningful to me, and I keep it handy for those moments when I want to stop terrorizing myself with my own thoughts. I am in charge of my thoughts, and I refuse to let scary thoughts overwhelm me. I ask Universal Love to help me work out all my problems. I am safe. All is well.

Love thy neighbor

AS THYSELF. We

often tend to

forget the last

two words.

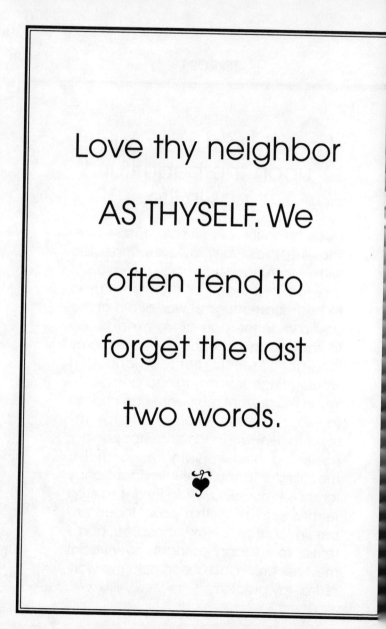

How can I be more compassionate?

This is a powerful time we live in, and we are definitely on the cutting edge of the forces that are going to help heal this planet. We are at a point right now where we can all go down the tubes or we can heal the planet. And it isn't up to "them," it's up to us, individually. Each morning when I wake up, I say to myself, "Help me to heal the planet today. I can love myself more. I can have less prejudice and less judgment today. I can let the love flow more. I can be more compassionate." There are so many little ways in which I can be helpful. I can make room for other cars on the freeway. I can be patient at crowded check-out counters. I can send postcards to leaders who act with compassion. I can cut out humorous cartoons and send them with my bills. I can send love to troubled areas. We are all one in Truth, so it is possible to go beyond competition, comparison, and judgment. Compassion is one of the highest forms of love. I look around myself. Everyone I see, myself included, is worthy of love.

Thoughts weave

the tapestry of

my life.

My thoughts are my best friends.

I used to fear my thoughts, for they made me so uncomfortable. I thought that I had no control over them. And then I learned that my thinking was creating my experiences and that I could choose to think any thought I wanted to. As I learned to take control of my thoughts and gently channel them in the directions I wanted them to go, my whole life began to change for the better. Now I know that I am the thinker that chooses the thoughts. The thoughts that I choose to think shape my life. Now if a negative thought pops up, I let it pass like a cloud on a summer day. I choose to release thoughts of resentment and shame and guilt. I choose to think thoughts of love and peace and joy and how I can help to heal the planet. My thoughts have become friends, and I enjoy thinking them.

I am never in a

hurry because I

have a lifetime

of time.

I have all the time in the world.

Time is exactly what I make it to be. If I choose to feel rushed, then time speeds up and I do not have enough of it. If I choose to believe there is always enough time for me to do the things I want to do, then time slows down and I accomplish what I set out to do. If I find myself stuck in traffic, I immediately affirm that all of us drivers are doing our best to get there as soon as we can. I take a deep breath and bless the other drivers with love and know that I will make my destination at the perfect time. When we can see the perfection of each experience, then we are never rushed or delayed. We are in the right place at the right time, and all is well.

I am in the most
wonderful transition
time, and I enjoy
every moment of it.

I am willing to change.

We are living in a transition time. It's a time of releasing old beliefs and of learning new ones. Loneliness, anger, isolation, fear, and pain are all part of the old fear syndrome, and that's really what we want to change. We want to move from fear into love. In the Piscean Age, we reached outside of ourselves and looked to other people to save us. In the Aquarian Age, which we're entering now, people are beginning to go within and find that they have the power to save themselves. This is a wonderful, liberating thing for us. Some people get frightened because it seems to be responsibility, but it is really our ability to respond to life, not in a victim way, but in a way that empowers us. It's a wonderful feeling when you don't have to be dependent on an outside person and to know that you have within you tremendous abilities to make positive changes in your life.

Put love into your trip. Love goes in every direction, so you know that everywhere you go, love is waiting for you.

I am a peaceful traveler.

Throughout the day, I check in on my body's tension level. No matter where I am, I take a moment to sit quietly, breathe deeply, and release any tension. I am totally in sync with life. My inner quest and my outer activities transport me from experience to experience. All is well. All forms of transportation that I use are safe — airplanes, trains, buses, cars, trucks, boats, sleds, skateboards, bicycles — all of them. When taking a trip, I prepare myself mentally by knowing I am always safe and secure. I arrange my belongings for easy access so I will feel organized and together, and I make my way joyfully toward my destination.

We trust that our next breath is there. Let's begin to trust that other things will be there for us, also.

I trust myself.

The world is a work of art, and so am I. For me to contribute positively to this ongoing creation, it is necessary that I trust the process of life. If things get difficult, I confidently go within and anchor my thoughts in Truth and love. I ask for the guidance of the Universe as I make my way safely through stormy seas and calm, blissful weather. My job is to stay in the present moment and to choose clear, simple, positive thoughts and words. I know it isn't necessary or even possible to have a reason for everything. I do know that I was born a beautiful and trusting soul. I take a moment now to treasure the mysterious and invisible process of life that I am.

Accept yourself totally and completely for one full day and see what happens.

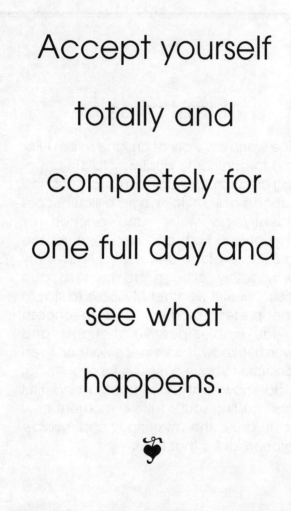

The love I give is the love I receive.

As I love and accept myself exactly as I am right here and right now with all my so-called flaws and embarrassing parts, I find it easier to accept you in the same way. When I put conditions on my love, for myself or others, then I am not loving freely. "I will love you if" is not love; it is control. So I learn to release the need to control others and allow them the freedom to be who they are. I see us all struggling on our pathways, learning to create peace inside of ourselves, doing the best we can with the understanding, knowledge, and awareness we have at the time. As more of us open our consciousness to work on the level of unconditional love, we will tap into the new level of spiritual power that is here for us. I see a blanket of benevolence covering the planet and helping us transform our consciousness from fear to love.

The more I

understand, the

more my world

expands.

I am constantly increasing my understanding.

I am teachable. Every day I open my awareness a little more to the Divine Wisdom within me. I am glad to be alive and so grateful for the good that has come to me. Life, to me, is an education. Every day I open my mind and my heart, as a child does, and I discover new insights, new people, new viewpoints, and new ways to understand what's happening around me and within me. My human mind may not always understand at first. Understanding seems to require lots of love and patience. My new mental skills are really helping me feel more at ease with all the changes in this incredible school of life here on Planet Earth.

In uniqueness

there is no

competition and

no comparison.

I am unique, and so is everyone else.

We are all one in Spirit. Yet, my face is a unique and different expression of the face of God. You and I are not supposed to be alike. While many people live their lives by what the neighbors think, I can choose to follow my own heart and let the neighbors think whatever they wish. I am neither too much nor too little, and I do not have to prove myself to anyone. I choose to cherish and love myself as the Divine, Magnificent Expression of Life that I am. Being me is an exhilarating adventure! I follow my inner star, and sparkle and shine in my own unique way. I love life!

Love always

dissolves violence.

I believe in the power of love.

Love goes deeper than violence. Love lives in the heart of every human being on this earth. Wherever there is violence on this earth, love is the deeper issue trying to be heard. I am learning to listen to this silent cry within every violent report. I believe in the tools of my mind, and with these tools I move out of bondage with respect to negative experiences and into new, positive possibilities. Many people have not been taught how to use their minds as creative instruments, so they live under whatever beliefs they were raised with. Beliefs are very powerful. People fight and kill to justify and protect their beliefs. And yet beliefs are only thoughts, and thoughts can be changed. I love myself; therefore, I no longer violate myself or anyone else with cruel thoughts, harsh criticism, or severe judgments. I love myself; therefore, I let go of all punishing thoughts. I love myself; therefore, I give up the victim role and the victimizer role wherever I might have played these out. I forgive myself and I forgive others.

I claim my

feminine power

now.

Wise women don't sing the blues.

One hundred years ago, an unmarried woman could only be a servant in someone else's home, usually unpaid. She had no status, no say in things, and had to take life as it was handed to her. In those days, yes, a woman needed a man to have a complete life. Even fifty years ago, the choices for an unmarried woman were narrow and limited. Today an unmarried American woman has the whole world in front of her. She can rise as high as her capabilities and her belief in herself. She can travel, choose her jobs, make good money, have lots of friends, and create great self-esteem. Yes there is much to learn. But women have been wanting to take their power back for a long time. Now, as there are more single women than single men, we have a new opportunity to grow. Let us make the most of it. If we do not have Mr. Right in our lives at the moment, we still can be Miss Right for ourselves.

I am awake to

the power of

my words.

I respect my mind and my mouth.

I pay attention to all my words, and I carefully select them, because I desire to create beautiful experiences. As a child I was taught to select words according to the rules of grammar. However, as an adult I've found that the rules of grammar continually change, and what was improper at one time is proper at another time, or vice versa. Grammar does not take into consideration the meaning of the word and how it affects my life. My thoughts and my words shape my life, like a potter shapes clay into a bowl, a vase, a dinner plate, or a teapot. I am the words I think and speak. I am beautiful. I am intelligent. I am loving and kind. My words are respected in the world.

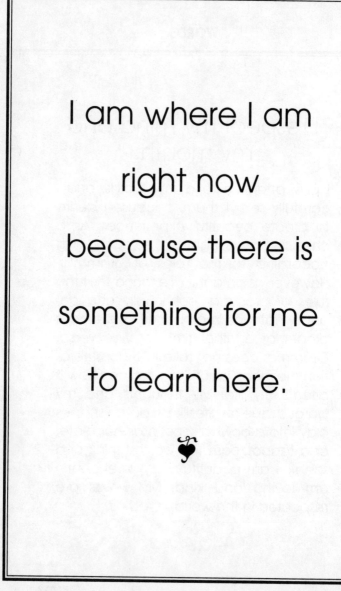

I am where I am
right now
because there is
something for me
to learn here.

My heart glows with pride when I think of the work I do.

I love getting up in the morning knowing I have important work to do today. My work is challenging and deeply fulfilling. I begin each day by blessing my current situation with love. I know that every day's work is only a stepping stone on my pathway and that I am where I am because of my thinking patterns. If I don't like where I am, I do the mental work to connect with Divine Wisdom deep within me where new doors are opening all the time. Here, I am always employed, always productive. I remember that there are millions of cells in my body employed 24 hours a day, performing wonderful work. As they go about their business, so do I go about my business of responding to the needs around me. My higher Power works through me as I work in the world.

I am comfortable

with my

self-worth.

I can do it!

The more I support myself with love and acceptance, the more worthy I feel. As I feel worthy, I feel better. In fact, I feel really good. I begin to let good things happen to me. I begin to see opportunities that I never saw before. I let life take me in new and interesting directions. I let my mind go beyond what I thought was possible. I become worthy of the totality of possibilities, and life suddenly becomes very exciting. I realize that I have a right to have the life I want. I might have to shift this or that, scrap an old belief, let go of an old limitation, but I can do it! YES! I am worthy. I am deserving of ALL GOOD!

I love myself

through all

experiences, and

all is well!

I value myself.

I've come a long way in my inner work on myself, and I still have much to do. I have learned that making myself "wrong" for anything is not a healing process. I can examine the situation and see where I could do it better next time. I can look for the thoughts that would support uncomfortable behavior and release them. When I become aware that I am making myself wrong for something, I can stop my punishing manner of thinking. Each day is a learning experience, and by our "mistakes" we learn how to do it differently next time. So I am never wrong. I am just learning. It is all so simple.

SELF-HELP RESOURCES

The following list of resources can be used for more information abo[ut] recovery options for addictions, health concerns, death and bereav[e]ment, and other issues. The addresses and telephone numbers listed are f[or] the national headquarters; look in your local yellow pages und[er] "Community Services" for resources closer to your area.

In addition to the following groups, other self-help organizations m[ay] be available in your area to assist your healing and recovery for a parti[c]ular life crisis not listed here. Consult your telephone directory, call a cou[n]seling center or help line near you, or contact:

Attorney Referral Network
(800) 624-8846

**National Self-Help
Clearinghouse**
25 West 43rd St., Room 620
New York, NY 10036
(800) 952-2075

***

AIDS

AIDS Hotline
(800) 342-2437

**Children with AIDS (CWA)
Project of America**
(800) 866-AIDS
(24-hour hotline)

**The Names Project -
AIDS Quilt**
(800) 872-6263

National AIDS Network
(800) 342-2437

Project Inform
19655 Market St., Ste. 220
San Francisco, CA 94103
(415) 558-8669

PWA Coalition
50 W. 17th St.
New York, NY 10011

Spanish AIDS Hotline
(800) 344-7432

**TDD (Hearing Impaired)
AIDS Hotline**
(800) 243-7889

ALCOHOL ABUSE

Al-Anon Family Headquarters
200 Park Ave. South
New York, NY 10003
(757) 563-1600

Alcoholics Anonymous (AA)
General Service Office
475 Riverside Dr.
New York, NY 10115
(212) 870-3400

**Children of Alcoholics
Foundation**
555 West 60th St., 5th Floor
New York, NY 10023
(212) 757-2100 ext. 6370
(212) 757-2208 (fax)
(800) 359-COAF

Meridian Council, Inc.
Administrative Offices
Elmcrest Terrace
Norwalk, CT 06850

**Mothers Against Drunk
Driving (MADD)**
(954) 690-6233

**National Association of
Children of Alcoholics (NACOA)**
11426 Rockville Pike, Ste. 100
Rockville, MD 20852
(301) 468-0985
(888) 554-2627

**National Clearinghouse for
Alcohol and Drug Information
(NCADI)**
P.O. Box 234
Rockville, MD 20852
(301) 468-2600

**National Council on Alcoholism
and Drug Dependency
(NCADD)**
12 West 21st St.
New York, NY 10010
(212) 206-6770

**National Council on
Alcohol & Drugs**
(800) 475-HOPE

Women for Sobriety
(800) 333-1606

***

ANOREXIA/BULIMIA

**American Anorexia/Bulimia
Association, Inc.**
293 Central Park West, Ste. 1R
New York, NY 10024
(212) 575-6200

Eating Disorder Organization
6655 S. Yale Ave.
Tulsa, OK 74136
(918) 481-4044

CANCER

National Cancer Institute
(800) 4-CANCER

ECAP (Exceptional Cancer Patients)
Bernie S. Siegel, M.D.
53 School Ground Rd., Unit 3
Branford, CT 06405
(203) 315-3321

***

CHILDREN'S ISSUES

Child Molestation

Adults Molested As Children United (AMACU)
232 East Gish Rd.
San Jose, CA 95112
(800) 422-4453

National Committee for Prevention of Child Abuse
332 South Michigan Ave.,
    Ste. 1600
Chicago, IL 60604
(312) 663-3520

Children's and Teens' Crisis Intervention

Boy's Town Crisis Hotline
(800) 448-3000
Covenant House Hotline
(800) 999-9999

Kid Save
(800) 543-7283

National Runaway and Suicide Hotline
(800) 448-3000

Youth Nineline
(Referrals for parents/teens about drugs, homelessness, runaways)
(800) 999-9999

Missing Children

Missing Children-Help Center
410 Ware Blvd., Ste. 400
Tampa, FL 33619
(800) USA-KIDS

National Center for Missing and Exploited Children
1835 K St. NW
Washington, DC 20006
(800) 843-5678

**Children with Serious Illnesses
(fulfilling wishes)**

Brass Ring Society
National Headquarters
551 East Semoran Blvd., Suite E-5
Fern Park, FL 32730
(407) 339-6188
(800) 666-WISH

Make-a-Wish Foundation
(800) 332-9474

***

CO-DEPENDENCY

Co-Dependents Anonymous
(602) 277-7991

***

DEATH/GRIEVING/SUICIDE

Grief Recovery Helpline
(800) 445-4808

Grief Recovery Institute
8306 Wilshire Blvd., Ste. 21A
Beverly Hills, CA 90211
(213) 650-1234

**National Hospice Organization
(NHO)**
1901 Moore St. #901
Arlington, VA 22209
(703) 243-5900

**National Sudden Infant
Death Syndrome**
Two Metro Plaza, Ste. 205
Landover, MD 20785
(800) 221-SIDS

Seasons: Suicide Bereavement
P.O. Box 187
Park City, UT 84060
(801) 649-8327

Share
(Recovering from violent death
of friend or family member)
100 E 8th St., Suite B41
Cincinnati, OH 45202
(513) 721-5683

Survivors of Suicide
Call your local Mental Health
Association for the branch
nearest you.

Widowed Persons Service
(202) 434-2260
(800) 424-3410 ext. 2260

DEBTS

Credit Referral
(Information on local credit
   counseling services)
(800) 388-CCCS

Debtors Anonymous
General Service Office
P.O. Box 400
Grand Central Station
New York, NY 10163-0400
(212) 642-8220

***

DIABETES

American Diabetes Association
(800) 232-3472

***

DRUG ABUSE

Cocaine Anonymous
(800) 347-8998

**National Cocaine-Abuse
Hotline**
(800) 262-2463
(800) COCAINE

**National Institute of Drug
Abuse (NIDA)**
Parklawn Building
5600 Fishers Lane, Room 10A-3
Rockville, MD 20852
(301) 443-6245 (for information)
(800) 662-4357 (for help)

World Service Office (CA)
3740 Overland Ave., Ste. C
Los Angeles, CA 90034-6337
(310) 559-5833
(800) 347-8998
(to leave message)

***

EATING DISORDERS

Eating Disorder Organization
6655 S. Yale Ave.
Tulsa, OK 74136
(918) 481-4044

Overeaters Anonymous
National Office
P.O. Box 44020
Rio Rancho, NM 87174-4020
(505) 891-2664

mblers Anonymous
tional Council on Compulsive
mbling
4 West 59th St., Room 1521
w York, NY 10019
2) 903-4400

***

ALTH ISSUES

heimer's Disease
ormation
0) 621-0379

nerican Chronic Pain
sociation
). Box 850
cklin, CA 95677
6) 632-0922

nerican Foundation of
aditional Chinese Medicine
5 Beach St.
n Francisco, CA 94133
5) 776-0502

nerican Holistic Health
sociation
). Box 17400
aheim, CA 92817
4) 779-6152

Chopra Center for Well-Being
Deepak Chopra, M.D.
7630 Fay Ave.
La Jolla, CA 92037
(619) 551-7788

The Fetzer Institute
9292 West KL Ave.
Kalamazoo, MI 49009
(616) 375-2000

Hippocrates Health Institute
1443 Palmdale Court
West Palm Beach, FL 33411
(561) 471-8876

Hospicelink
(800) 331-1620

Institute for Noetic Sciences
P.O. Box 909, Dept. M
Sausalito, CA 94966-0909
(800) 383-1394

**The Mind-Body
Medical Institute**
185 Pilgrim Rd.
Boston, MA 02215
(617) 632-9525

**National Health Information
Center**
P.O. Box 1133
Washington, DC 20013-1133
(800) 336-4797

Optimum Health Care Institute
6970 Central Ave.
Lemon Grove, CA 91945
(619) 464-3346

**Preventive Medicine
Research Institute**
Dean Ornish, M.D.
900 Bridgeway, Ste. 2
Sausalito, CA 94965
(415) 332-2525

World Research Foundation
20501 Ventura Blvd., Ste. 100
Woodland Hills, CA 91364
(818) 999-5483

***

HOUSING RESOURCES

Acorn
(Nonprofit network of low- and
    moderate-income housing)
739 8th St., S.E.
Washington, DC 20003
(202) 547-9292

***

IMPOTENCE

Impotence Institute of America
10400 Patuzent Pkwy, Ste. 485
Washington, DC 20006
(800) 669-1603

INCEST
**Incest Survivors Resource
Network International, Inc.**
P.O. Box 7375
Las Cruces, NM 88006-7375
(505) 521-4260 (Hours:
Mon. – Sat., 2 – 4 P.M. and
11 P.M. –Midnight /Eastern time)

***

PET BEREAVEMENT

Bide-A-Wee Foundation
410 E. 38th St.
New York, NY 10016
(212) 532-6395

The Animal Medical Center
510 E. 62nd St.
New York, NY 10021
(212) 838-8100

**Holistic Animal Consulting
Center**
29 Lyman Ave.
Staten Island, NY 10305
(718) 720-5548

***

RAPE/SEXUAL ISSUES

Austin Rape Crisis Center
1824 East Oltorf
Austin, TX 78741
(512) 440-7273

tional Council on Sexual
dictions and Compulsivity
)0 S. Northchase Parkway,
Suite 200
1th Marietta, GA 30067
0) 989-9754

**kually Transmitted Disease
ferral**
0) 227-8922

***

IOKING ABUSE

:otine Anonymous
8 Greenwich St.
1 Francisco, CA 94123
5) 750-0328

***

OUSAL ABUSE

**tional Coalition Against
mestic Violence**
). Box 34103
ishington, DC 20043-4103
2) 544-7358

**tional Domestic Violence
•tline**
0) 799-SAFE

**

STRESS REDUCTION

**The Biofeedback &
Psychophysiology Clinic**
The Menninger Clinic
P.O. Box 829
Topeka, KS 66601-0829
(913) 350-5000

New York Open Center
(In-depth workshops to
    invigorate the spirit)
83 Spring St.
New York, NY 10012
(212) 219-2527

Omega Institute
(A healing, spiritual retreat
    community)
260 Lake Dr.
Rhinebeck, NY 12572-3212
(914) 266-4444 (info)
(800) 944-1001 (to enroll)

Rise Institute
P.O. Box 2733
Petaluma, CA 94973
(707) 765-2758

The Stress Reduction Clinic
Center for Mindfulness
University of Massachusetts
    Medical Center
55 Lake Ave. North
Worcester, MA 01655
(508) 856-1616
(508) 856-2656

******

We hope you enjoyed this Hay House book.
If you would like to receive a free catalog
featuring additional Hay House books and
products, or if you would like information
about the Hay Foundation, please contact:

Hay House, Inc.
P.O. Box 5100
Carlsbad, CA 92018-5100

or call:
(800) 654-5126
(800) 650-5115 (fax)

Please visit the Hay House Website at:
www.hayhouse.com